TROMBONE

FILM FAVORITES

Solos and Band Arrangements
Correlated with Essential Elements® Band Method

Arranged by
MICHAEL SWEENEY, JOHN MOSS and PAUL LAVENDER

Welcome to ESSENTIAL ELEMENTS FILM FAVORITES! The arrangements in this versatile book can be used either in a full concert band setting or as solos for individual instruments. The SOLO pages appear at the beginning of the book, followed by the BAND ARRANGE-MENT pages. The supplemental CD recording or PIANO ACCOMPANIMENT book may be used as an accompaniment for solo performance.

ISBN 978-0-634-08701-1

HAL•LEONARD®
CORPORATION
7777 W. BLUEMOUND RD. P.O. BOX 13819 MILWAUKEE, WI 53213

00860151

PIRATES OF THE CARIBBEAN

(A medley including: The Medallion Calls • The Black Pearl)

TROMBONE
Solo

Music by KLAUS BADELT
Arranged by MICHAEL SWEENEY

00860151

From the Paramount and Twentieth Century Fox Motion Picture TITANIC

MY HEART WILL GO ON

(Love Theme From 'Titanic')

Music by JAMES HORNER
Lyric by WILL JENNINGS
Arranged by JOHN MOSS

TROMBONE
Solo

00860151

From THE LORD OF THE RINGS: THE FELLOWSHIP OF THE RING

MAY IT BE

TROMBONE
Solo

**Words and Music by EITHNE NI BHRAONAIN,
NICKY RYAN and ROMA RYAN**
Arranged by JOHN MOSS

00860151

From Walt Disney Pictures' TARZAN™

YOU'LL BE IN MY HEART

TROMBONE
Solo

Words and Music by
PHIL COLLINS
Arranged by MICHAEL SWEENEY

00860151

From the Motion Picture SHREK 2

ACCIDENTALLY IN LOVE

TROMBONE
Solo

Words and Music by
ADAM F. DURITZ
Arranged by MICHAEL SWEENEY

Moderate Rock

Featured in the Motion Picture 2001: A SPACE ODYSSEY

ALSO SPRACH ZARATHUSTRA

By RICHARD STRAUSS
Arranged by MICHAEL SWEENEY

TROMBONE
Solo

00860151

From the Paramount Motion Picture MISSION: IMPOSSIBLE

MISSION: IMPOSSIBLE THEME

TROMBONE
Solo

By LALO SCHIFRIN
Arranged by MICHAEL SWEENEY

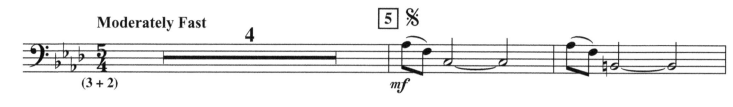

From SHREK

MUSIC FROM SHREK

(A medley including: Fairytale Opening • Ride The Dragon)

TROMBONE
Solo

Music by JOHN POWELL
and HARRY GREGSON-WILLIAMS
Arranged by JOHN MOSS

00860151

From the TriStar Motion Picture THE MASK OF ZORRO
ZORRO'S THEME

TROMBONE
Solo

Composed by
JAMES HORNER
Arranged by JOHN MOSS

Heroically

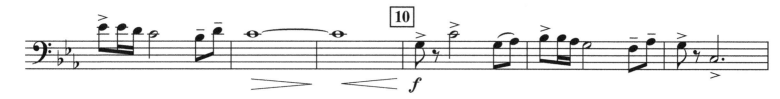

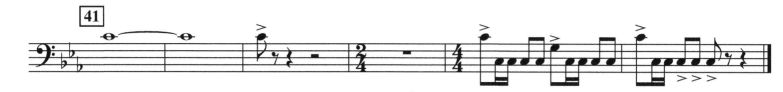

PIRATES OF THE CARIBBEAN

(A medley including: The Medallion Calls • The Black Pearl)

TROMBONE
Band Arrangement

Music by KLAUS BADELT
Arranged by MICHAEL SWEENEY

00860151

From the Paramount and Twentieth Century Fox Motion Picture TITANIC

MY HEART WILL GO ON

(Love Theme From 'Titanic')

TROMBONE
Band Arrangement

Music by JAMES HORNER
Lyric by WILL JENNINGS
Arranged by JOHN MOSS

From THE MUPPET MOVIE
THE RAINBOW CONNECTION

TROMBONE
Band Arrangement

Words and Music by
PAUL WILLIAMS and KENNETH L. ASCHER
Arranged by PAUL LAVENDER

00860151

From THE LORD OF THE RINGS: THE FELLOWSHIP OF THE RING

MAY IT BE

TROMBONE
Band Arrangement

**Words and Music by EITHNE NI BHRAONAIN,
NICKY RYAN and ROMA RYAN**

Arranged by JOHN MOSS

00860151

From Walt Disney Pictures' TARZAN™

YOU'LL BE IN MY HEART

TROMBONE
Band Arrangement

**Words and Music by
PHIL COLLINS**
Arranged by MICHAEL SWEENEY

Moderately

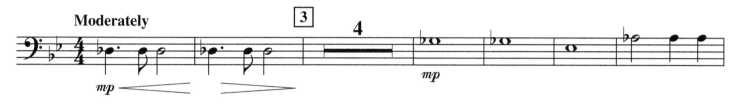

From the Motion Picture SHREK 2

ACCIDENTALLY IN LOVE

Words and Music by
ADAM F. DURITZ
Arranged by MICHAEL SWEENEY

TROMBONE
Band Arrangement

Featured in the Motion Picture 2001: A SPACE ODYSSEY

ALSO SPRACH ZARATHUSTRA

TROMBONE
Band Arrangement

By Richard Strauss
Arranged by MICHAEL SWEENEY

From the Paramount Motion Picture MISSION: IMPOSSIBLE

MISSION: IMPOSSIBLE THEME

By LALO SCHIFRIN
Arranged by MICHAEL SWEENEY

TROMBONE
Band Arrangement

Moderately Fast
(3 + 2)

From SHREK
MUSIC FROM SHREK
(A medley including: Fairytale Opening • Ride The Dragon)

TROMBONE
Band Arrangement

Music by JOHN POWELL and HARRY GREGSON-WILLIAMS
Arranged by JOHN MOSS

00860151

From the TriStar Motion Picture THE MASK OF ZORRO

ZORRO'S THEME

TROMBONE
Band Arrangement

Composed by JAMES HORNER
Arranged by JOHN MOSS

Copyright © 1998 TSP Music, Inc.
This arrangement Copyright © 2004 TSP Music, Inc.
All Rights Administered by Sony/ATV Music Publishing, 8 Music Square West, Nashville, TN 37203
International Copyright Secured   All Rights Reserved

MORE FAVORITES FROM ESSENTIAL ELEMENTS

These superb collections feature favorite songs that students can play as they progress through their string method books. Each song is arranged to be played by either an orchestra or by soloists, with optional accompaniment on CD.

Each song appears twice in the book, featuring:
- Solo instrument version
- String arrangement for orchestra or ensembles
- Accompaniment CD included with conductor's score
- Accompaniment CD available separately
- Piano accompaniment book that is compatible with recorded backgrounds

Available:
- Conductor
- Violin
- Viola
- Cello
- String Bass

- Accompaniment CDs
- Value Starter Pak
  (includes 24 Student books
  plus Conductor Book w/CD

CHRISTMAS FAVORITES
Arranged by Lloyd Conley
Songs include:
The Christmas Song
  (Chestnuts Roasting
  on an Open Fire)
Frosty the Snow Man
A Holly Jolly Christmas
Jingle-Bell Rock
Let It Snow! Let It Snow! Let It Snow!
Rockin' Around the Christmas Tree
We Wish You a Merry Christmas

BROADWAY FAVORITES
Arranged by Lloyd Conley
Songs include:
Beauty and the Beast
Cabaret
Edelweiss
Get Me to the Church on Time
I Dreamed a Dream
Go Go Go Joseph
Memory
The Phantom of the Opera
Seventy Six Trombones

MOVIE FAVORITES
Arranged by Elliot Del Borgo
Includes themes from:
An American Tail
Chariots of Fire
Apollo 13
E.T.
Forrest Gump
Dances with Wolves
Jurassic Park
The Man from Snowy River
Star Trek
Mission: Impossible

PATRIOTIC FAVORITES
Arranged by John Moss
Songs include:
America, the Beautiful
Battle Hymn of the Republic
God Bless America
Hymn to the Fallen
My Country, 'Tis of Thee (America)
The Patriot
The Star Spangled Banner
Stars and Stripes Forever
This Is My Country
Yankee Doodle

FOR MORE INFORMATION, SEE YOUR LOCAL MUSIC DEALER,
OR WRITE TO:

HAL•LEONARD®
C O R P O R A T I O N
7777 W. BLUEMOUND RD. P.O. BOX 13819 MILWAUKEE, WI 53213

Visit Hal Leonard Online at **www.halleonard.com**

Prices, contents, and availability subject to change without notice.
Some products may not be available outside the U.S.A.

0210